Thriving Downtowns:

Stategies for Small Town Renewal and Revitalization

HARLAN G. OTIS

OTIS
PUBLISHING

Contents

Introduction   1

Chapter 1: Economic Development Initiatives   3

Chapter 2: Cultural and Social Programming   6

Chapter 3: Infrastructure Improvements   8

Chapter 4: Strategies for Small Town Revitalization   11

Chapter 5: Successful Revitalization Efforts   16

Conclusion   20

Introduction

Picture yourself strolling down a vibrant Main Street, where every storefront is bustling with activity, and the air resonates with the buzz of community interactions. This image encapsulates the heart and soul of small-town revitalization. Main Streets serve not only as economic hubs but also as the lifeblood of community identity and heritage. The revival of these central spaces can transform towns, creating environments where businesses thrive, residents engage, and visitors feel welcomed.

Revitalizing a downtown area requires a multifaceted approach encompassing economic, cultural, and social elements. In this short ebook, we delve into ten transformative strategies designed to reignite the vitality of these essential urban arteries. From fostering economic growth through local business incentives to celebrating cultural heritage with community events, each chapter presents actionable insights and real-world examples illustrating the potential for renewal.

Economic strategies are crucial for revitalizing Main Streets. Towns can create dynamic economic ecosystems by attracting new businesses, supporting existing ones, and enhancing local entrepreneurship. Additionally, infrastructure improvements, such as better public transportation and pedestrian-friendly spaces, significantly make downtown areas more accessible and appealing.

Cultural and social vitality is equally important. Hosting festivals, promoting the arts, and preserving historical landmarks help foster a sense of community pride and belonging. Learning from successful revitalization projects, this ebook offers a comprehensive guide to implementing these strategies, ensuring that small towns can flourish as vibrant, attractive, and economically robust spaces.

Chapter 1: Economic Development Initiatives

Attracting and Retaining Businesses

Revitalizing Main Streets is not just a dream but a tangible possibility. Economic development initiatives, such as startup grants, low-interest loans, and tax incentives, can attract and retain businesses that are the backbone of our town's economy. 'Shop local' campaigns can foster a community-focused consumer base, supporting our local merchants and craftspeople. These efforts, when combined, create a sustainable economic environment that boosts local commerce and reinforces the town's uniqueness and appeal.

Towns can implement policies that encouragelong-term business stability to further support these initiatives. Offering reduced rent for the first few years, providing marketing support, and creating networking opportunities can significantly enhance business retention.

3

Moreover, establishing partnerships with local chambers of commerce and economic development organizations can provide businesses with access to additional resources and advocacy, ensuring they have the support needed to thrive.

Developing Incubation Centers

Another dynamic aspect of economic revitalization includes the development of incubation centers for small businesses. These centers offer crucial resources such as shared spaces, technology access, and professional guidance, lowering the barriers for new entrepreneurs and fostering a collaborative business community. Such initiatives help cultivate a culture of innovation and entrepreneurship and weave a tight-knit network of local businesses that drive economic growth and job creation.

Incubation centers can also serve as hubs for training and education, providing workshops on business management, marketing, and financial planning. By collaborating with local universities and technical schools, these centers can offer valuable internships and hands-on learning experiences for students, further enriching the local talent pool. Additionally, successful businesses that emerge from incubation centers can serve as inspiring case studies, demonstrating the potential for growth and success within the community.

Integrating Historical Restoration

Integrating historical restoration into downtown revitalization efforts not only preserves a town's cultural heritage but also adds economic value. Restored historic buildings can attract tourists, new residents, and businesses looking for unique, character-filled spaces. Grants and tax credits aimed explicitly at historical preservation can ease the financial burden of restoration projects for property owners. These incentives make it feasible to maintain the architectural integrity of historic sites while adapting them for modern uses.

Community engagement is essential in these projects. Involving local historians, residents, and business owners in the planning process ensures that restoration efforts reflect the town's heritage and meet the community's needs. Hosting events in newly restored buildings can generate excitement and draw attention to the revitalization efforts, fostering a sense of pride and ownership among residents. This blend of preservation and modernization can create a vibrant, economically robust downtown that honors its past while looking toward the future.

Chapter 2: Cultural and Social Programming

Hosting Community-Driven Events

Beyond economics, the cultural and social revitalization of Main Streets plays a significant role in rekindling the community spirit and enhancing the quality of life for residents and visitors alike. Integrating cultural and social programming involves hosting community-driven events such as festivals, art shows, farmers' markets, and holiday celebrations that spotlight local traditions and crafts. These events serve as both a celebration of local heritage and a catalyst for economic activity, drawing visitors from beyond the local community and providing markets for local artisans and producers.

To further enrich these events, towns can introduce thematic celebrations that reflect the community's unique identity. For example, a town known for its apple orchards could host an annual Apple Festival featuring local produce, apple-themed crafts, and live music. Interactive workshops and demonstrations, such as pottery making or traditional cooking classes, can also be incorporated, offering participants hands-on experiences and deeper connections to local culture. Such events generate revenue and strengthen the social fabric by bringing residents together in shared activities.

Leveraging Unique History and Culture

Programming that leverages the town's unique history and culture can transform Main Streets into vibrant showcases of community pride and creativity. For example, historical reenactments, heritage walks, museum nights, entertainment, and education deepen communal ties to the town's history, attracting tourism and fostering a sense of belonging among residents.

In addition, collaborating with local schools and historical societies to develop educational programs can enrich community engagement. Students can participate in projects exploring the town's history and contribute to exhibits or performances showcased during community events. Utilizing digital platforms, such as virtual tours and online archives, can also broaden the reach of these programs, making the town's heritage accessible to a broader audience. By intertwining education with entertainment, towns can create dynamic, informative experiences that honor the past while inspiring future generations.

Chapter 3: Infrastructure Improvements

Enhancing Accessibility and Safety

Revitalizing Main Streets requires a comprehensive approach to infrastructure enhancements that prioritize accessibility, safety, and aesthetic appeal. Key improvements include the development of pedestrian-friendly sidewalks that accommodate individuals of all mobility levels, ensuring that pathways are wide, well-maintained, and equipped with curb cuts and tactile paving. Adequate street lighting is crucial, not only for safety but also for creating a welcoming atmosphere during evening hours. High-quality, energy-efficient lighting can reduce crime rates and enhance the overall sense of security.

Well-maintained public areas, such as parks and plazas, provide spaces for social interaction and community events, contributing to the vibrancy of the downtown area. Preserving historical architecture is equally important, as it maintains the town's unique character and heritage. Efforts to restore and preserve historical buildings can involve careful attention to architectural details and the use of materials and techniques consistent with the original construction.

The installation of public art and the beautification of street landscapes through the addition of green spaces, planters, and street furniture can significantly enhance the visual appeal of Main Streets. These aesthetic improvements elevate the visitor experience and foster a sense of local pride and community ownership.

Investing in Smart Infrastructure

Investing in 'smart' infrastructure is a forward-thinking approach that can significantly enhance the functionality and appeal of Main Streets. 'Smart' infrastructure involves the integration of digital technology and data analytics into the physical infrastructure, making it more efficient, sustainable, and user-friendly. For instance, providing free public Wi-Fi in downtown areas lets residents and visitors stay connected, encouraging more extended visits and increased patronage of local businesses.

Electric vehicle charging stations are another critical feature, promoting sustainable transportation options and attracting ecoconscious visitors. Interactive informational kiosks can provide valuable information about local attractions, historical sites, and upcoming events, enriching the visitor experience and making the area more navigable.

Additional intelligent features may include sensor-based waste management systems that optimize waste collection routes, reducing operational costs and improving cleanliness, and smart lighting systems that adjust brightness based on real-time data to conserve energy. By integrating these advanced technologies, Main Streets can become more adaptive and resilient, meeting contemporary urban needs while preserving their historical significance.

Chapter 4: Strategies for Small Town Revitalization

Leveraging the Main Street Approach™

The Main Street Approach™, a practical and adaptable framework for community-based revitalization initiatives, is a crucial strategy we will explore. It focuses on transforming downtown areas by leveraging local assets, fostering public-private partnerships, and engaging the community. This approach promotes economic vitality, enhances the area's physical appearance, and improves residents' overall quality of life, making it a valuable tool for small-town revitalization.

Implementing Smart Growth Strategies

Innovative growth strategies help small towns and rural communities achieve sustainable development. These approaches emphasize mixed-use development, walkable neighborhoods, and inclusive community engagement. Walkable neighborhoods are designed to be pedestrian-friendly, with amenities such as shops, schools, and parks within walking distance of residential areas. This design can enhance the quality of life for residents, as it promotes physical activity, reduces traffic congestion, and fosters a sense of community. By integrating land use planning with transportation, housing, and environmental policies, small towns can create vibrant, resilient communities that attract new businesses and residents.

Activating the Public Realm

Creating active and inviting public spaces is crucial for downtown revitalization. This can be achieved by developing parks, plazas, and pedestrian-friendly streetscapes. Public art installations, outdoor seating areas, and community events can also draw people to the area and foster a sense of community. These efforts make the downtown area more attractive to both residents and visitors.

Establishing Revolving Loan Funds

Revolving loan funds provide financial assistance to small businesses and property owners looking to invest in the downtown area. These funds can be used for building renovations, facade improvements, and other revitalization projects. By offering low-interest loans or grants, communities can stimulate private investment and encourage economic growth.

Creating Business Incubators and Co-Working Spaces

Business incubators and co-working spaces support local entrepreneurs and small businesses by providing affordable office space, resources, and mentorship. These facilities foster innovation and collaboration, helping new businesses get off the ground and thrive. By nurturing a vibrant business ecosystem, small towns can attract and retain talent, leading to long-term economic prosperity.

Creating a Unified Branding and Marketing Campaign

Developing a cohesive branding strategy for the downtown area can enhance its identity and attract visitors. This includes creating a logo, tagline, and consistent messaging across all marketing materials. Collaborative marketing efforts with local businesses, such as hosting joint events or cross-promotions, can further boost visibility and drive traffic to the area.

Encouraging Residential Development

Introducing or enhancing residential options within the downtown area can bring a steady flow of people who live, work, and
play locally. This can include renovating the upper floors of
commercial buildings into apartments or lofts and incentivizing
new housing developments. A vibrant residential community
supports local businesses and adds to the area's overall vitality.

Historic Preservation and Adaptive Reuse

Preserving our history and finding new uses for old structures is
not just a strategy but a commitment to our community's
unique character. Adaptive reuse can transform vacant or
underutilized buildings into thriving centers for business,
culture, and com- munity activities. This strategy not only
saves on demolition costs but also attracts heritage tourism,
reminding us of our rich past and promising future.

Strengthening Local Arts and Culture

Investing in arts and cultural programs can significantly
enhance the attractiveness of downtown areas. This can include

public art installations, murals, art festivals, and supporting local theaters or music venues. A strong cultural scene can draw visitors, encourage community participation, and create a vibrant, creative atmosphere.

Developing Transportation and Accessibility Improvements

Enhancing transportation options and improving accessibility can make downtown areas more attractive and convenient. This includes expanding public transit services, creating bike lanes, improving sidewalks, and ensuring ADA compliance. Better connectivity and accessibility encourage more people to visit and spend time in the downtown area, supporting local businesses and activities.

Chapter 5: Successful Revitalization Efforts

Greenville, South Carolina

Reflecting on successful examples provides tangible insights into the effective revitalization of Main Streets. Consider the transformation of Main Street in Greenville, South Carolina. Through a combination of public and private investments, Greenville transformed its once-dilapidated Main Street into a bustling avenue lined with local businesses, green spaces, and art installations. The city's strategy included widening sidewalks, adding bike lanes, and fostering a vibrant arts scene, which helped attract new businesses and tourists.

Baker City, Oregon

Another exemplary case is the revitalization of Main Street in Baker City, Oregon. Through comprehensive planning that included infrastructure improvements, cultural programming, and economic incentives, Baker City rejuvenated its historic Main Street into a dynamic hub of commerce and culture. The town now hosts numerous events throughout the year that celebrate its rich heritage and attract visitors from across the region, contributing significantly to its economy.

Additional Examples

Container Park in Las Vegas, Nevada

This project repurposed shipping containers into a vibrant space featuring restaurants, boutique shops, and entertainment venues. It transformed a previously underutilized area into a popular community hub, showcasing how innovative design can revitalize downtown areas.

Downtown Project in Las Vegas, Nevada

This comprehensive effort aimed to create a thriving urban environment by investing in small businesses, technology startups, and real estate. It included creating community spaces, promoting arts and culture, and improving safety, contributing significantly to the revitalization of downtown Las Vegas.

High Line in New York City, New York

The High Line transformed an abandoned elevated railway into a linear park featuring gardens, walkways, and public art installations. This project revitalized the surrounding neighborhoods and became a significant tourist attraction, demonstrating the power of urban green spaces in downtown revitalization.

Pike Place Market in Seattle, Washington

Known for its vibrant atmosphere and historic significance, Pike Place Market underwent extensive renovations to preserve its charm while enhancing accessibility and safety. The revitalization efforts included updating infrastructure, adding new vendor spaces, and creating public gathering areas, boosting the market's appeal to both locals and tourists.

Gaslamp Quarter in San Diego, California

This historic district was transformed from a neglected area into a lively entertainment district through strategic preservation and development. The project included restoring Victorian buildings, improving streetscapes, and encouraging a mix of dining, shopping, and cultural experiences, making it a key destination in downtown San Diego.

Conclusion

In this short book, we have explored ten key strategies for revitalizing downtown areas, each illustrated with real-world examples. These strategies form a comprehensive approach to rejuvenating small towns, providing a roadmap to economic growth and community engagement. By applying these methods, towns can breathe new life into their Main Streets, transforming them into thriving hubs of activity.

Fostering economic growth is a critical aspect of downtown revitalization. This can be achieved through initiatives that attract new businesses, support local entrepreneurs, and create job opportunities. Additionally, celebrating cultural identity plays a significant role in making Main Streets more inviting and inclusive. Incorporating local traditions, hosting cultural events, and promoting diversity can significantly enhance the community's appeal and vibrancy.

Infrastructure enhancement is another vital strategy involving improving and modernizing public spaces, transportation systems, and utilities. These upgrades not only make the area more accessible and appealing but also support the overall func- tionality and sustainability of the downtown district. Learning from successful revitalization projects, both locally and globally, provides valuable insights and inspiration, enabling towns to adopt best practices and tailor them to their unique needs.

Together, these strategies create a tapestry of potential for small towns. By implementing economic, cultural, and infrastructural improvements, towns can ensure that their Main Streets survive and thrive as dynamic, attractive, and economically robust spaces. The collective impact of these efforts will lead to lasting revitalization, fostering a sense of pride and community among residents and visitors alike.

About the Author

Harlan G. Otis is a life-long learner and an enthusiast of new experiences. With a passion for exploring diverse intellectual pursuits, he writes on a variety of subjects including multi-language learning, healthcare, finance, and business strategies. Harlan's writing aims to inspire and educate readers, offering deep insights and practical advice drawn from his own con- tinuous journey of discovery and personal growth. His work reflects a commitment to expanding knowledge and fostering a deeper understanding of the world around us.

Also by Harlan G. Otis

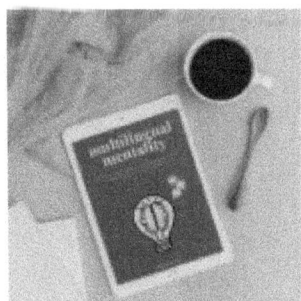

Multilingual Mentality:
Strategies for Learning Multiple
Languages Simultaneously

Introducing the essential guide
that will not only **accelerate your
language acquisition** but also
transform the way you view
learning languages forever.

'Multilingual Method: Strategies for Learning Multiple
Languages Simultaneously' is your passport to unlocking
the secrets behind fast, effective language learning.

www.ingramcontent.com/pod-product-compliance
Lightning Source LLC
Chambersburg PA
CBHW071036050426
42335CB00050B/1797